Usborne Art ideas
Drawing
Faces

INTERNET-LINKED

Rosie Dickins and Jan McCafferty

Designed and illustrated by Jan McCafferty, Doriana Berkovic,
Nicola Butler, Non Figg and Cristina Adami

Managing Editor: Fiona Watt
Managing Designer: Mary Cartwright

Consultants: Miles Jefcoate and Gill Figg
U.S. Editor: Carrie Seay

Additional illustrations by Kathy Ward, Ian McNee, Katrina Fearn and Anna Milbourne
Photographs by Howard Allman
Image manipulation: John Russell

Internet links

This book is a self-contained beginner's guide to drawing faces. You do not need a computer to enjoy it, but if you would like to find out more about drawing, there are brief descriptions of useful Web sites throughout the book. The best way to visit these Web sites is to go to the Usborne Quicklinks Web site at **www.usborne-quicklinks.com** Here, you will find direct links to all the Web sites listed. If you have any problems using the Internet, the guidelines on this page will help you.

What you need

The Web sites listed in this book can be accessed with a standard home computer and an Internet browser (the software that enables you to display information from the Internet). Here's a list of the basic requirements:

- A PC with Microsoft® Windows® 95, Windows® 98 or Windows® 2000, or a Macintosh PowerPC with Operating System 8 or later versions
- 64Mb RAM
- A browser such as Microsoft® Internet Explorer 4, or Netscape® Navigator 4, or later versions
- Connection to the Internet via a modem (preferably 56Kbps) or a faster digital or cable line
- An account with an Internet Service Provider (ISP)
- A sound card to hear sound files

Extras

Some Web sites need additional programs, called plug-ins, to play sounds or to show videos and animations. If you do not have the necessary plug-in, a message saying so will appear on the screen. There is usually a button on the site that you can click on to download the plug-in. Alternatively, go to Usborne Quicklinks and click on **Net Help** for links to download plug-ins. Here is a list of plug-ins that you might need:
QuickTime – lets you play video clips.
Shockwave® – lets you play animations.
RealPlayer® – lets you play videos and sound files.

Site availability

Occasionally you may get a message saying a site is unavailable. This may be temporary, so try again a few minutes later. Some Web site addresses may change or sites may close down. The links in Usborne Quicklinks are regularly updated to send you to the right place. If a site is no longer available, we will replace it, if possible, with another suitable site.

Downloadable pictures

Selected pictures, clip art and templates from this book can be downloaded from the Usborne Quicklinks Web site free of charge, for your own personal use. The pictures must not be copied or distributed for any commercial or profit-related purpose. To find these pictures, go to the Usborne Quicklinks Web site and follow the instructions there.

★ The downloadable pictures are all marked with this star symbol, to identify them.

Internet safety

All the Web sites in this book have been selected by Usborne editors as suitable, in their opinion, for a general audience, although no guarantees can be given and Usborne Publishing is not responsible for the accuracy or suitability of the information on any Web site other than its own. We recommend that children are supervised while on the Internet and that they do not use Internet Chat Rooms.

Very rarely, an unsuitable site might be reached accidentally by typing in an address wrongly. To avoid this possibility, we strongly recommend that all the Web sites listed in this book are accessed through the Usborne Quicklinks Web site.

Computer viruses

A computer virus is a program that can damage your computer. A virus can get into your computer when you download programs from the Internet, or in an attachment (an extra file) that arrives with an e-mail. You can buy anti-virus software at computer stores or download it from the Internet. To find out more about viruses, go to the Usborne Quicklinks Web site and click on **Net Help**.

Getting to the sites

The quickest way to reach all the Web sites described in this book is to go to Usborne Quicklinks at: **www.usborne-quicklinks.com** and follow the simple instructions you find there.

A COMPUTER IS NOT ESSENTIAL
TO USE THIS BOOK
This guide to drawing faces
is a complete, self-contained
book on its own.

Contents

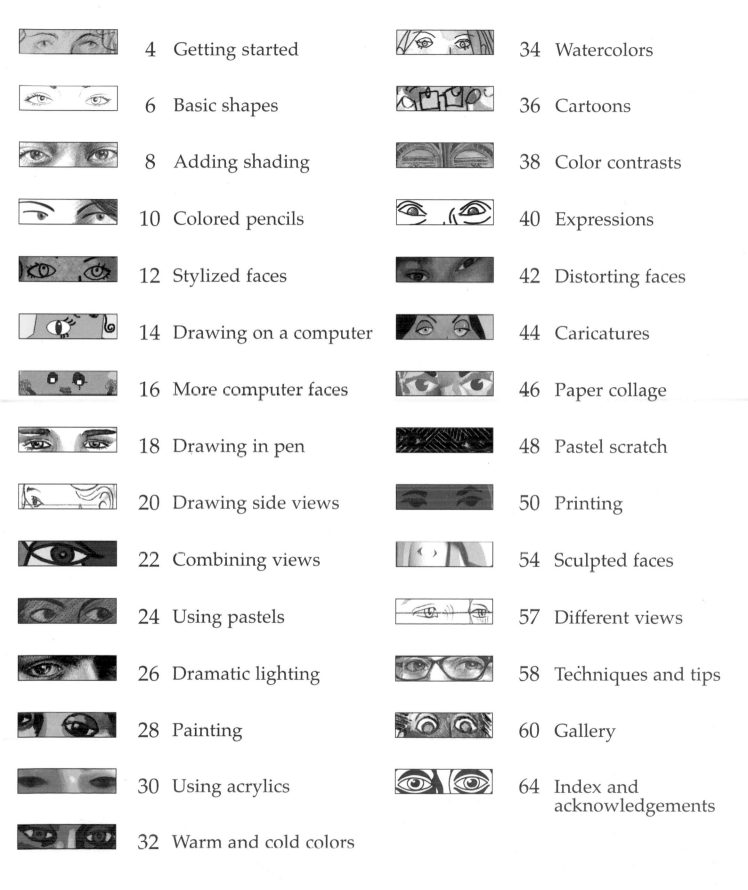

Getting started

Faces are fascinating to draw, and there are lots of ways to draw them. This book covers a range of methods and materials, from pastels and paints to paper collage but to start with, you only need pencil and paper.

Find out about keeping a sketchbook to practice drawing in at: **www.arts.ufl.edu/art/rt_room/sketchbk/sketching.html** For a quick link to this site, go to: **www.usborne-quicklinks.com**

Collecting pictures

When you are drawing faces, it's useful to have pictures for reference. Collect pictures and photographs of faces – you will need them for some of the projects in this book. Keep them in a folder with your drawings.

This book begins with drawing in pencil, then goes on to show you how to use lots of different materials.

Try using different materials together, such as pen and watercolors (see page 36).

Try drawing stylized faces (see pages 12-13) as well as realistic ones.

Collect postcards of pictures by famous artists from museums and art galleries.

Cut out pictures from magazines.

Styles

In this book you'll find lots of drawing styles. You can also get ideas from looking at pictures in museums or on the Internet.

This face was printed. You can find out how on pages 50-53.

This face was drawn in pastels. Find out more on pages 26-27.

This stylized face was colored with tissue paper. See how on pages 12-13.

👁 Explore different artists' styles with the Art Detective at: **www.edu web.com/pintura/index.html** For a quick link to this site, go to: **www.usborne-quicklinks.com**

5

Basic shapes

Although no two faces are exactly the same, all faces have the same basic shapes. These shapes are shown on the photograph below. Follow the steps on these pages to draw a face using guidelines.

👁 Find out more about basic face shapes at: **www.sanford-artedventures.com/create/tech_face_shapes.html** For a quick link to this site, go to: **www.usborne-quicklinks.com**

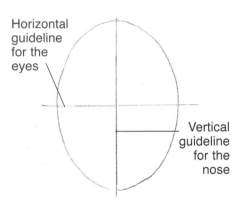

Horizontal guideline for the eyes

Vertical guideline for the nose

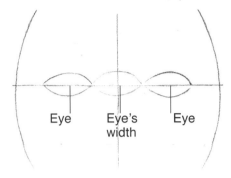

Eye

Eye's width

Eye

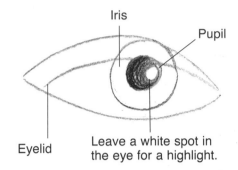

Iris

Pupil

Eyelid

Leave a white spot in the eye for a highlight.

1. Draw an oval in pencil. Add a faint line down the middle of the oval. Add another faint line across the middle.

2. Draw two almond shapes for the eyes. Position them on the horizontal guideline, an eye's width apart.

3. Draw a circle in each almond, for the iris. Add an overlapping line for the eyelid. Draw a small circle for the pupil and fill it in.

The distances and guidelines marked on this photograph work for almost every face.

★ You can download a template showing all these guidelines from **www.usborne-quicklinks.com**

4. Draw the lashes and eyebrows. Make your pencil lines follow the direction in which the hairs grow.

The eyes are halfway down.

The base of the nose is halfway between the eyes and chin.

The nose is halfway across.

The eyes are halfway between the side of the face and the nose.

The corners of the mouth line up with the middles of the eyes.

The nose is as wide as the gap between the eyes.

Mark the base halfway between the eyes and chin.

5. The nose is on the vertical guideline. Draw a triangle for the basic nose shape. Add three overlapping circles at the base.

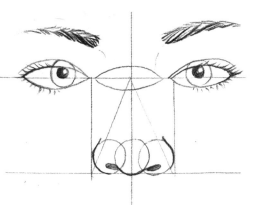

Find out how to shade your drawing on page 9.

6. Outline the circles to make the sides and bottom of the nose. Add two oval shapes for the nostrils and fill them in.

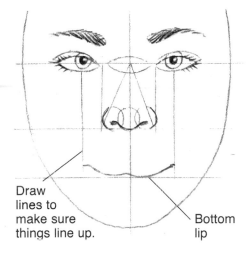

Draw lines to make sure things line up.

Bottom lip

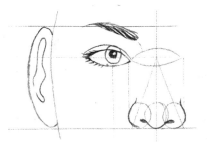

Add lines for the neck and shoulders.

You can erase the guidelines when you have finished.

7. Draw the bottom lip halfway between the nose and chin. Make the corners line up with the middles of the eyes.

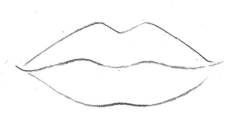

8. Draw a flattened-out 'm' shape for the top lip. Add another flatter 'm' shape for the line between the lips.

9. Draw the ears, making them level with the eyebrows at the top and the nose at the bottom. Add a curved shape inside each.

10. Draw the hairline above the eyebrows. Then, draw the rest of the hair, making your lines follow the way the hair falls.

Adding shading

Once you have drawn a basic face shape, you can try adding shading. This creates the highlights and shadows that make your drawing look three-dimensional.

 To see a gallery of shaded pencil portraits, go to: **www.pencilportraits.co.uk/index2.htm**, click on "Gallery" and then on the index numbers to view pictures. For drawing tips, click on "How you can start drawing Pencil Portraits". For a quick link to this site, go to: **www.usborne-quicklinks.com**

Light and dark pencil shading

Pencil is good for shading because it's easy to make it lighter or darker. When you shade, use the side of your pencil's lead and do lots of parallel lines, close together. Press gently for light shading. For dark shading, press firmly and go over an area several times.

Pencils come in varying degrees of softness, shown as an 'H' or 'B' number on the side of the pencil. H stands for hard and B stands for black.

An HB pencil is a medium hardness pencil. It is good for drawing outlines and doing light shading.

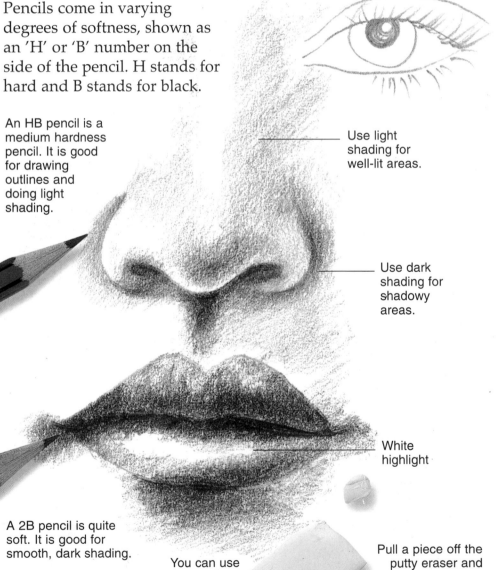

Use light shading for well-lit areas.

Use dark shading for shadowy areas.

White highlight

A 2B pencil is quite soft. It is good for smooth, dark shading.

You can use a soft putty eraser to create white highlights.

Pull a piece off the putty eraser and roll it between your fingers. Dab it over your drawing to lift off the pencil.

Shading textures

Skin is usually smooth. For smooth shading, press gently and build up dark tones slowly. For a very smooth effect, blend your pencil marks by rubbing them with a fingertip or cotton swab, but don't overdo this.

Smooth shading

Blended shading

Hair and clothes often have rough textures. You can use dots and lines to create textured shading.

Use short lines for rough, hairy skin or fabric.

Use criss-cross lines for a woven texture.

Use dots for freckled skin or stubbly hairs.

Use squiggly lines for curly hair or furry fabric.

8

Shading your drawing

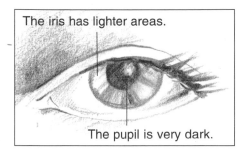

The iris has lighter areas.

The pupil is very dark.

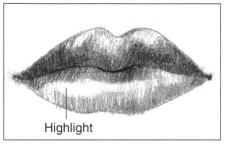

Highlight

1. Shade around the eye with a 2B pencil. Then, shade the iris with lines coming out from the pupil. Shade the pupil, leaving a tiny, white highlight.

2. Shade the lips with short pencil strokes, making the top lip darker than the bottom one. Use an eraser to add a highlight on the bottom lip.

3. Add dark shading around the base of the nose. Lightly shade the sides of the nose. At the top, blend this shading into the shading around the eyes.

4. Shade around the tip of the nose, leaving a highlight on the tip itself. Shade the creases at the corners of the mouth and the hollow underneath it.

5. Shade lightly around the edge of the face and add a dark shadow under the chin. Then, fill in the hair with wispy pencil lines.

Lightly shade the neck, too.

9

Colored pencils

Colored pencils are good for making delicately colored drawings. You can use them to create either textured or smooth areas of color – the drawing on the right uses both. The artist, David Hockney, has contrasted the smooth shading on the man's face and tie with the rough, sketchy shading in the background. The face on the next page also uses smooth shading, with a contrasting texture in the hair.

👁 For tips on using colored pencils, go to: **www. crayola-europe.com/tech/colored_ pencils.html** For a quick link to this site, go to: **www.usborne-quicklinks.com**

Color shading

Shading with colored pencils is similar to shading with ordinary pencils (see page 8). The strength of a color depends on how hard you press. You can also blend different colors together by shading them on top of each other. Some colored pencils are water-soluble. This means that their lead dissolves in water (see below).

Manolo, London, by David Hockney. This pencil drawing uses just two colors – red and blue.

If you press hard, you get a dark, strong color.

If you press lightly, you get lighter, softer colors.

Use criss-cross lines, dots and squiggles to create texture on clothes.

Add blue to make colors darker – this dark brown is a blend of light brown and blue.

Water-soluble pencils can be blended with water for a soft, painted look.

For delicate skin tones, press gently as you shade and build up colors gradually.

This pinkish skin tone is a blend of orange, yellow and brown.

This olive color is a blend of brown, green and orange.

To use water-soluble pencils, dip a brush in water and paint over your shading.

10

Colored pencil drawing

For this project, you can use normal colored pencils or water-soluble pencils without any water. This style of drawing is often used for fashion designs, so look through some fashion magazines for some ideas and different faces to draw.

The highlights in the eyes were left uncolored.

You can add touches of pink on the cheeks.

Use a strong color on the lips to look like lipstick.

1. Draw an oval in light blue pencil. Don't press too hard. Then, add the features. Try drawing the irises to the right, so the eyes look sideways.

2. Draw the hair in light blue. Draw around the sides of the face and one side of the nose in brown. Add the eyebrows.

3. Sharpen the brown pencil and draw dark lines along the top of the eyes. Draw in the irises and pupils with sharp pencils, too.

4. Lightly shade the face in light brown. Add some darker brown down one side of the face and under the chin.

5. Shade the lips in red. Add brown on the top lip, to make it darker. Fill in the hair with long, flowing pencil lines.

Stylized faces

A stylized face is a face that has been simplified or has parts which have been exaggerated. The steps below show you how to draw a stylized, stretched face with simple features.

👁 A famous artist named Modigliani painted many people with stylized faces. You can see some of his pictures by going to: **www.ibiblio.org/wm/paint/auth/modigliani/ modigliani.boy.jpg** or: **www.ibiblio.org/wm/paint/auth/ modigliani/modigliani.girl-polka-dot-blouse.jpg** For quick links to these sites, go to: **www.usborne-quicklinks.com**

Drawing a stretched face

Draw faint guidelines to help you.

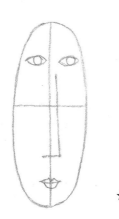

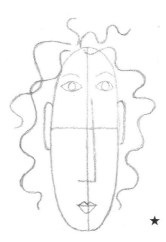

1. Draw a long oval shape in pencil. Add almond-shaped eyes about a quarter of the way down the oval.

2. Draw a long, straight nose ending about three-quarters of the way down. Add a small mouth below.

3. Draw long, thin ears about half-way down the oval. Add the eyebrows and wavy lines for the hair.

4. Draw over the face in pen. Leave it for a few minutes, for the pen to dry. Then, erase the pencil lines.

A tissue-paper face

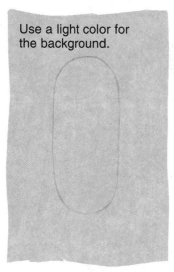
Use a light color for the background.

Use a different color for each new shape.

1. Cut out a rectangle of tissue paper. Glue it onto a piece of white cardboard. Draw an oval in the middle.

2. For the face, tear out a piece of tissue paper about the size of your oval. Glue the tissue over the oval.

3. Tear out a rough rectangle of tissue for the shoulders. Glue it below the oval. The shapes can overlap.

4. Tear out a piece of tissue for the hair. It can be any rough shape. Glue it at the top of the oval.

12

Experiment with different face shapes and hairstyles.

Add extra pieces of tissue for lips, cheeks or earrings.

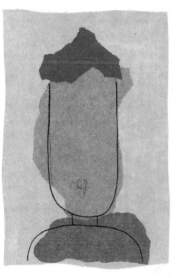

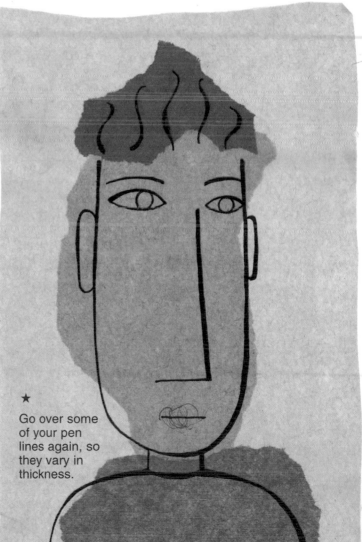

Go over some of your pen lines again, so they vary in thickness.

5. When the glue is dry, draw around the face in pen. Add a curve for the body and two lines for the neck.

6. Use a pen to draw stylized features and hair. You don't have to follow the tissue-paper shapes exactly.

Drawing on a computer

Drawing on a computer is a good way to experiment with colors and shapes. Most computers have a program that lets you make drawings. The projects in this book use a program called Microsoft® Paint, but most drawing programs work in a similar way.

Microsoft® Paint

To find Paint, move the pointer over *Start* in the corner of your screen. Click the left mouse button. A list appears. Move the pointer up the list to *Programs* and click. A new list appears. Move across to *Accessories* and click. You should see *Paint* on the list that appears. Move the pointer over *Paint* and click again to open it.

In Paint, you will see a tool box at the side of the screen and a paint box at the bottom. The tool box controls the kind of mark you make. The paint box controls the color. To select a tool or color, move your pointer over one of the squares and click the left mouse button.

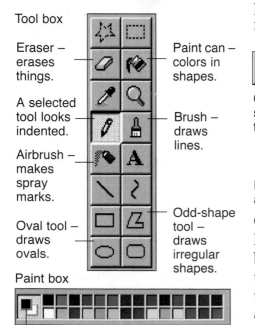

Tool box

Eraser – erases things.

Paint can – colors in shapes.

A selected tool looks indented.

Brush – draws lines.

Airbrush – makes spray marks.

Oval tool – draws ovals.

Odd-shape tool – draws irregular shapes.

Paint box

This box shows you which color you have chosen.

Lines and shapes

Brush

To draw a line, click on the brush tool. Hold down the left mouse button and move the pointer to draw.

Oval tool

The pointer started here.

The further you move the pointer, the bigger the oval gets.

For an oval, click on the oval tool. Hold down the left mouse button and move the pointer. Finish the oval by releasing the button.

Odd-shape tool

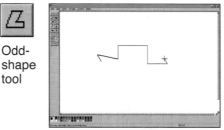

Each time you move the pointer and click, a new line appears.

Click on the odd-shape tool. Hold down the left mouse button and move the pointer to draw the first line. Release the button. Move the pointer and click. A new line appears, joined to the first. Click twice to complete the shape.

Filling in

Paint can

Make sure the tip of the paint drip is inside the shape.

The shape must have an unbroken outline, or the color will leak out.

To fill in a shape with color, click on the paint can tool and on a color. Move the pointer over your shape and click again to color it in.

Airbrush

To spray a color, first click on the airbrush tool. Then, click on a color. Hold down the left mouse button and move the pointer to make spray marks.

Made a mistake?

Eraser

You can erase things with the eraser tool. Click on the tool. Hold down your left mouse button and move your pointer over what you want to erase.

Computer cartoons

These steps show you how you can use simple lines and shapes to draw a cartoon-style face in Paint. There are some more ideas for computer drawings on the next two pages.

To see lots of examples of what you can draw on a computer, visit the Children's Computer Painting Museum at: **www.yk.rim.or.jp/~hyper01/indexe.htm** Click on the "museum entrance" and visit the different rooms. For a quick link to this site, go to: **www.usborne-quicklinks.com**

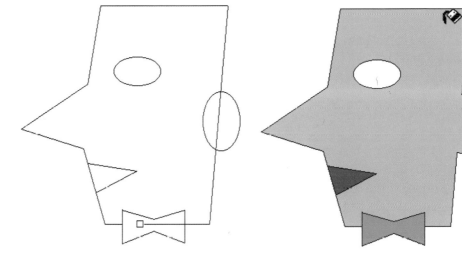

1. Click on the odd-shape tool. Draw a rectangular head with a pointy nose. Add a bow tie. Then, draw a triangular shape for the mouth.

2. Use the oval tool to add an eye and an ear. Then, click on the eraser tool and erase the lines inside the bow tie and on the side of the ear and mouth.

3. Click on the paint can tool and a color in the paint box. Fill in the face. Fill in the mouth and bow tie in different colors. Leave the eye white.

Start each oval slightly to the side of where you want it to be.

4. Click on the oval tool. Then click on a color in the paint box. Draw small ovals inside the eye and ear, then fill them in with the paint can.

5. Click on the brush tool and on white. Draw a highlight on the eye. Click on black. Draw curly hair, eyelashes, an eyebrow and a moustache.

6. Fill in the background color with the paint can. Click on the airbrush tool and on red. Add touches of red on the nose and cheeks.

More computer faces

There are lots of different effects you can create when drawing faces on a computer. Here are some more ideas to try for faces with different features, hair and expressions. All these faces were drawn using Microsoft® Paint (see page 14).

👁 To get a real illustrator's tips on how to draw faces and bodies using a computer, go to: **www.sillybilly.com/draw1.html** For a quick link to this site, go to: **www.usborne-quicklinks.com**

★You can download these faces separately to use as clip art from **www.usborne-quicklinks.com**

Try using the shape tools to draw features.

You can use the airbrush tool for fluffy hair.

You can use the brush tool to draw curly or zigzag hair.

Funny face

1. Click on the paint can tool and on a color from the paint box. Click on the background to fill it with that color.

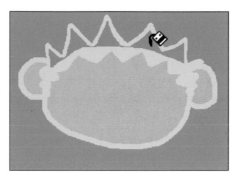

2. Click on the brush tool and a different color. Draw a face with spiky hair. Fill the hair and face with colors.

3. Click on the brush tool and a new color. Draw in the eyes. Choose another color and draw the nose and mouth.

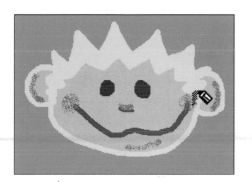

4. Click on the airbrush and another color. Spray touches of color on the nose, cheeks and chin, and on the ears.

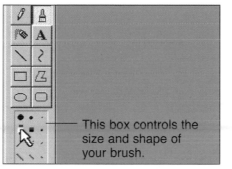

This box controls the size and shape of your brush.

5. Click on the brush tool. A box appears below the tool box. Click on the biggest square, then click on white.

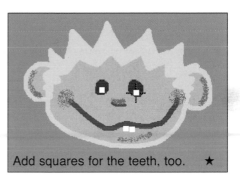

Add squares for the teeth, too. ★

6. Move the pointer over an eye. Click the left mouse button once to add a square. Add one to the other eye, too.

Airbrush face

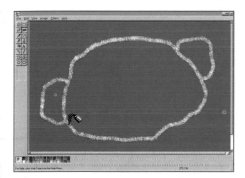

1. Use the paint can to fill the background with a dark color. Then, click on the airbrush tool and a light color. Spray a rounded face shape. Add ears.

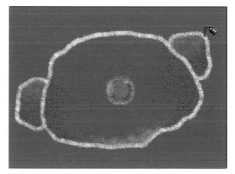

2. Color parts of the face with the airbrush. Use different, bright colors like blue, green, red and orange. For strong shading, go over an area several times.

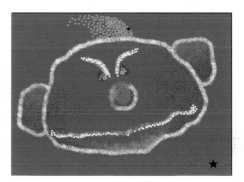

3. Spray the eyes and mouth. Select a square brush tool (see step 5 above). Add squares of color for the hair and eyes by clicking on and off the left mouse button.

Drawing in pen

If you want to create bold, striking drawings, pens are an excellent choice. They are simple to use, but give clear lines and strong colors. Drawing in pen is a challenge, too, because you can't erase anything.

Different pens

You can buy special art pens, but you can draw with any kind of pen on most kinds of paper. Experiment with art pens and ballpoint pens as well as fountain pens and felt-tip pens.

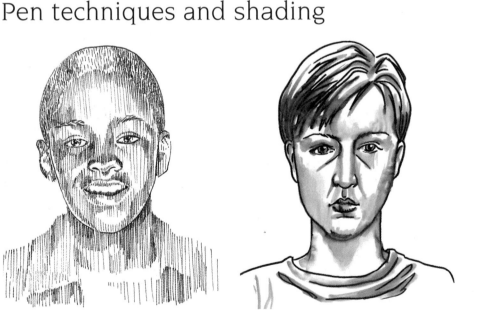

Fountain pen – can be used with different colors of ink.

Ballpoint pen – produces a thin, even line.

Felt-tip pen – good for adding color.

Art pen – gives a smooth, controlled line.

👁 See how to use pen lines for various styles of shading at: **www.homeschoolarts.com/pi-l1-2.htm** To read more, click on the pencil saying "Next Page". For a quick link to this site, go to: **www.usborne-quicklinks.com**

Different kinds of pen can be used with other materials for a range of effects. Some of these effects are shown below.

Pen techniques and shading

★ Pen drawing

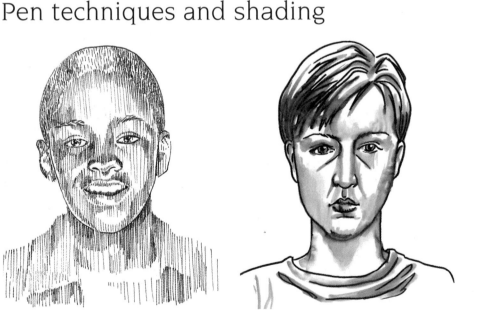

★ Smudged pen shading

★ Pen painted over with watercolors

Unlike pencil lines, pen strokes don't get lighter or darker, or blend together. With pen, you create dark shading by making marks close together. For light shading, make marks further apart. For highlights, leave blank areas.

Most felt-tip pens contain ink that dissolves in water. This ink "bleeds" when it gets wet, so you can use it to create smudged shading. Draw a face in felt-tip pen. Wet a brush and paint water over the top, as explained on the next page.

Ballpoint pens and some art pens contain permanent ink (ink that won't dissolve in water). Use these pens if you want to paint over your picture without it smudging. This kind of ink stains, so be careful not to get it on your clothes.

18

Self-portrait with smudged pen

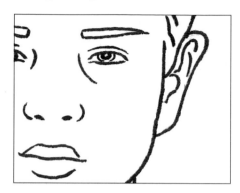

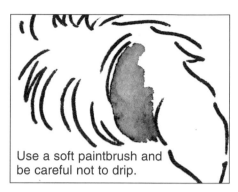

Use a soft paintbrush and be careful not to drip.

1. Looking closely in a mirror, draw your face in black felt-tip pen on thick, white paper.

2. Draw the basic shapes of your features, but don't add small details or shading.

3. Dip a brush in water. Paint over your pen lines to dissolve the ink, starting with the hair.

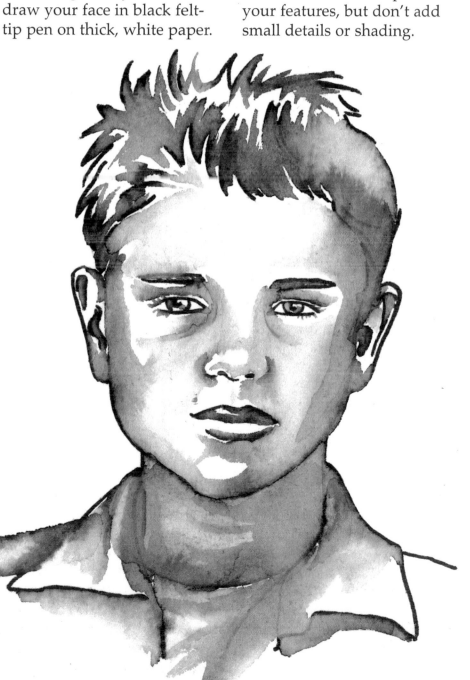

4. As the ink dissolves, spread it out with your brush to fill in the dark areas.

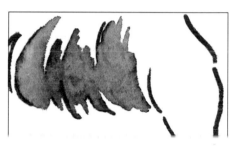

5. The further you spread the ink, the lighter it becomes. Wet your brush again if you need to.

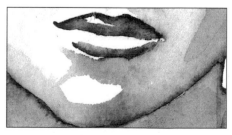

6. For highlights, leave the paper unpainted so the white of the paper shows through.

19

Drawing side views

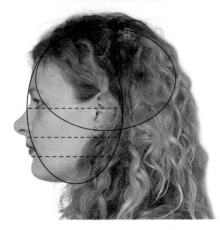

A side view, or profile, of a face looks quite different from a front view. These pages show you how to draw a side view using guidelines, and how to make silhouettes.

> 👁 Find out how to draw cartoon-style profiles at: **www.polykarbon. com/tutorials/newface/profile1.htm** Click on "Next" to see the rest of the steps. For a quick link to this site, go to: **www.usborne-quicklinks.com**

A side view

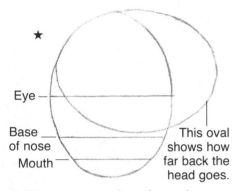

Eye —

Base of nose

Mouth

This oval shows how far back the head goes.

1. Draw an oval and mark horizontal guidelines for the eye, nose and mouth (see page 6). Draw a second oval, the same size, on its side like this.

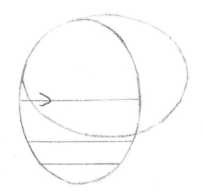

2. For the eye, draw a 'v' shape on its side. Position the 'v' on the guideline for the eye, about a quarter of the way across the first oval.

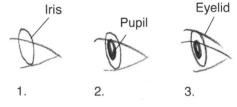

Iris

Pupil

Eyelid

1.   2.   3.

Shade the pupil, leaving a small, white highlight.

3. Draw an oval for the iris of the eye, making it overlap the top of the 'v'. Add an oval pupil. Draw a line at the top of the iris, for the eyelid.

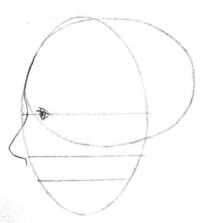

4. Draw the forehead, making it curve inward level with the eye. Add the nose, making the base of the nose level with the guideline for the nose.

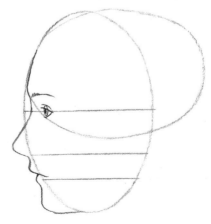

5. Draw the lips and chin next. The lower lip slopes back slightly from the upper one. Then, draw in the eyebrow over the eye.

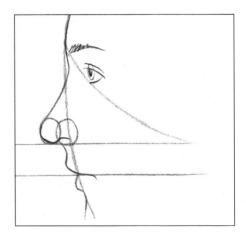

6. Draw two overlapping circles at the base of the nose. Draw a line from the left circle curving up across the second circle, to form the nostril.

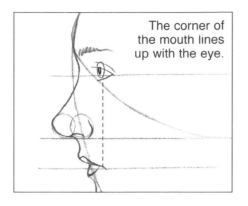

The corner of the mouth lines up with the eye.

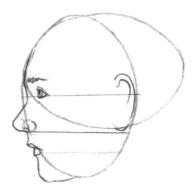

7. Draw the mouth with two curved lines for the lips. The top lip is thinner than the lower lip. Add a line slanting down between the lips.

8. For the ear, draw a curved shape at the edge of the first oval. The ear lines up with the eyebrow and nose. Add a line inside the top of the ear.

9. Draw a hollow inside the ear. Add the hair and neck. Erase your guidelines and carefully go over the main lines of your drawing again.

Silhouettes

A good way to compare different people's profiles is to make silhouettes (cut-out shapes) like the ones shown below.

1. Tape some paper to a wall with masking tape. Sit a friend in front of it. Place a lamp so the profile casts a shadow on the paper.

2. Draw around the shadow in pencil. Then, take the paper down and carefully cut around the shape you have drawn.

Try making silhouettes of other friends in different colors. Put them together like this to compare them.

Combining views

Most portraits only show one view of a person's face, but you can create a striking effect by combining different views. The picture on the left is a good example. It was painted by a famous Spanish artist named Pablo Picasso.

Picasso's picture shows his model, Dora Maar, from the side and the front at the same time. For instance, the nose sticks out like a profile but you can see both nostrils, like in a front view. The bright colors make the face even more striking.

You can try making your own picture with combined views by following the steps at the bottom of these pages.

👁 To see pictures by Picasso, including this portrait of Dora Maar and similar paintings, go to the On-line Picasso Project at: **www.tamu.edu/ mocl/picasso/tour/tg37.html** The site is in English, although the names of the pictures are given in French. Scroll down the list and click on an image to see a larger version. For a quick link to this site, go to: **www.usborne-quicklinks.com**

Portrait of Dora Maar, by Pablo Picasso

Picture with combined views

This project combines two views of a face, a front view and a side view, starting with two separate drawings. You can see how to draw a front view on pages 6-7. For help with drawing a side view, turn back to pages 20-21.

1. Fold a large piece of paper in half. On the left, draw a front view of a face using guidelines. Extend the guidelines across the paper. On the right, draw a side view of the same face at the same size.

Use thin, watery paint to tint the newspaper shapes.

2. Cut out the features and hair from both drawings. Mix up the pieces. Draw an oval on a new piece of paper. Glue the pieces onto it.

3. Copy the outlines of the put-together face on a new piece of paper. Simplify the features and straighten the lines.

4. Draw extra lines between some of the features, to break up the face into shapes. Go over all the lines with a felt-tip pen.

5. Trace some of the shapes onto newspaper. Cut them out and glue them on. Paint the shapes in different colors.

Using pastels

If you want to make colorful drawings, pastels are ideal. You can use pastels in lots of ways, creating smooth blends of color or textured effects with dots, dabs and lines.

For tips on using oil pastels, go to: **www.sanford-artedventures.com/create/try_this_color_pastel.html** and click on "Technique Tips: Oil Pastels". Discover a pastel portrait by artist, Mary Cassatt at: **www.kidsart. com/IS/431.html** For quick links to these sites, go to: **www.usborne-quicklinks.com**

About pastels

There are two kinds of pastels: oil pastels and chalk pastels. Oil pastels are slightly sticky. Chalk pastels are powdery and easy to smudge. Pastels break easily, so keep them in a box when you are not using them.

Oil pastel

Blend oil pastels by shading colors on top of each other.

You can buy textured paper (sometimes called Ingres paper) made especially for pastels.

From a distance, dots of different colors seem to blend together.

Ordinary drawing paper is fine for pastels. It gives a smoother effect than Ingres paper.

Chalk pastel

Brown paper and colored paper work well with pastels.

Use either side of brown paper with oil pastels. For chalk pastels, use the rough side.

Chalk pastels need to be "fixed" (see page 59).

Blend chalk pastels by smudging them with your finger or a cotton swab.

Use the tip of a pastel for drawing fine lines.

Break a pastel in two and use the side for broad strokes.

Oil pastel face

For this picture, you will need oil pastels and a piece of colored paper. The color shows through the pastel marks and makes your finished picture look brighter. Oil pastels can be messy, so cover your table with newspaper before you begin.

Press firmly with your pencil.

Don't worry about being neat.

1. Draw a long, oval face in pencil. Make the nose extra long and connect it to one eyebrow at the top.

2. Add lines down the middle of the chin and neck. Color the face with slanting lines of yellow pastel.

3. Add brown lines on one side of the face, mixed with some more yellow. Use slanting, brown lines for the hair, too.

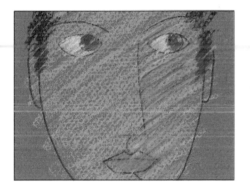

4. Fill in the whites of the eyes. Make the irises brown. For the lips, do short, slanting lines of pink.

5. Color the background light blue and the shoulders green. Add lines of white on the left and dark blue on the right.

Finish your drawing by going over the original pencil lines with a brown pastel.

Dramatic lighting

Lighting can completely change how someone looks – all-round lighting makes a face look flat, while side lighting, shown below, casts strong shadows and can make a face look mysterious. Black and white chalk pastels are good for drawing this dramatic lighting effect.

A famous 17th-century artist named Rembrandt painted many self-portraits using dramatic side lighting. You can see some of them at: **www.ibiblio.org/wm/paint/ auth/rembrandt/self/** Click on a picture to see a larger version of it. For a quick link to this site, go to: **www. usborne-quicklinks.com**

1. Find a picture of a face with strong lighting on one side, or ask a friend to pose for you, with a desk lamp shining toward one ear.

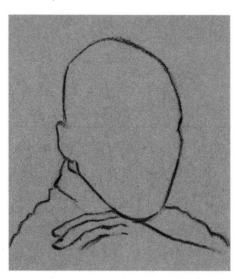

2. On a piece of beige or gray paper, use the tip of a black pastel to outline the head and shoulders, making them fill the paper.

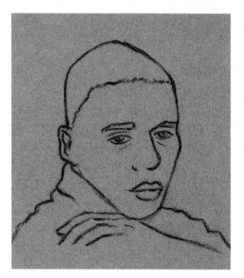

3. Draw in the features with the tip of the pastel. If you make a mistake, you can erase it with a putty eraser or smudge it away.

4. Break off a small piece of pastel and use the side of it to shade around the dark side of the face, down the side of the nose and under the mouth.

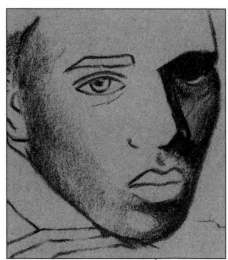

5. Shade lightly around the light side of the face. Where you stop, rub the shading with a fingertip so it blends with the color of the paper.

6. Shade lightly around the eye, nose and mouth on the light side of the face. Shade the upper lip so it is just slightly darker than the paper.

7. Add a little white pastel on the light side of the face, on the cheek and forehead. Rub the white pastel so it blends with the paper.

8. Shade the background and hair with strokes of black pastel. Let the strokes overlap the dark side of the face, so it blends into the shadows.

9. Add dark details, like the lashes and nostrils, with the tip of the black pastel. Add white highlights in the eyes, and on the nose and lips.

You will need to fix your picture (see page 59), to keep it from smudging.

The fingers have white highlights on top and dark lines underneath. There is a shadow on the back of the hand.

27

Painting

You can use paints to color faces drawn in pencil or pen, or try drawing faces directly in paint. The projects in this book use two kinds of paints: acrylics and watercolors. Acrylic paints give a different effect because they are much thicker than watercolors.

Acrylics work well on cardboard.

Thick Bristol paper is ideal for painting.

You can buy special paper to use with watercolors.

Paints and papers

You don't have to buy lots of colors of paint. To get started, you need red, yellow and blue. If you are using acrylics, you also need white. Whether you are using watercolors or acrylics, it is best to paint on thick paper as thin paper wrinkles when it gets wet.

You can get different reds, yellows and blues. The ones below are best for mixing other colors.

Crimson red

Cadmium yellow

Cobalt blue

Brushes

Brushes come in different sizes and textures. It's best to have a thick, a thin and a medium brush. Use soft brushes with watercolors. Hard brushes are good for acrylics.

Use a medium-size brush for drawing outlines and filling in skin and hair.

For painting small details, like the eyes, use a thin brush.

A thick brush is best for painting large areas, such as the background or clothes.

Cleaning up

Always clean your brushes after painting. Rinse them with water and, if they are stained, a little soap. Dry them with a cloth and pinch the bristles into shape.

Pinch the bristles of your brush into shape while they are damp.

Store brushes upright in a mug or jar, so the bristles don't get bent.

Mixing colors

Red, yellow and blue are called primary colors. You can't mix these colors yourself, but you can make most other colors by mixing them together.

👁 Find out about colors at: **www.sanford-art edventures.com/play/color1/color1.html** Click on "Let's go" and follow the pages to see how to mix colors. For a quick link to this site, go to: **www.usborne-quicklinks.com**

Mix red and yellow to make orange.

Mix blue and yellow to make green.

Mix red and blue to make purple.

Mix red, yellow and blue to make brown.

Making colors lighter and darker

To lighten acrylics, add white. To make watercolors lighter, thin them with water so the white of the paper shows through.

This green acrylic was lightened with white.

This green watercolor was lightened by adding water.

To make a color darker, add a little blue or brown. It's best not to use black paint as it makes some colors look dirty.

This yellow acrylic was darkened with brown.

This brown watercolor was darkened with blue.

Mixing skin tones

1. To mix a pinkish skin tone, dip your brush in some red paint. Dab the paint onto a mixing plate.

2. Add another dab of red. Add two dabs of yellow and one of blue. Mix them together with your brush.

3. Slowly add your mixture to white until you have the tone you want. For olive skin, you need less red, and for dark skin, more blue. Experiment until you get the right color.

Mix colors with a brush on a palette or an old plate.

Pinkish

Olive

Dark

Using acrylics

Acrylics are good for painting faces because they give bright, solid colors. They dry quickly and, once dry, you can paint over them and touch up details neatly.

> 👁 To see lots of acrylic paintings, go to: **www.liquitex. com/gallery/** and click where it says "Click here" to change the picture. For handy hints on using acrylics, go to: **www.liquitex. com/** Click on "tip of the month" and "Tips Archive". For quick links to these sites, go to: **www.usborne-quicklinks.com**

About acrylics

Acrylics are thick paints. You mix them with water to make them thinner. While they are wet, you can mix different colors. Once they are dry, however, they form a plastic skin and won't mix any more.

Use a brush with stiff bristles.

This face was copied from a picture with clearly divided skin tones.

• Acrylics dry quickly, so it's best not to squeeze out a lot of paint at once.

• Don't let acrylics dry on your brush or it will be hard to clean.

• If your acrylics are drying out too quickly, mix them with some water or sprinkle your mixing plate with water every 15 minutes.

• You can keep paint wet for a few hours if you cover your mixing plate with plastic foodwrap.

Cleaning up

Acrylics will wash off your brushes and plate easily when wet, so clean up quickly. If you get any paint on your clothes, rinse it off quickly with cold water. (It's a good idea to wear an old shirt.) If any paint dries onto your plate, you can scrape it off.

1. Find a picture in a magazine where you can see clear areas of different skin tones, like this one.

2. Draw over the magazine picture to divide the face into areas showing the three main skin tones and highlights.

3. Make a pencil drawing of the face on a new piece of paper. Include the lines you drew in step 2.

This face was painted with acrylic paints on white cardboard.

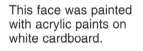

The shoulder was painted with the same skin tones as the face.

4. Mix paint to match the three main skin tones. Paint the areas with the darkest tone first. Then paint the medium and light tones.

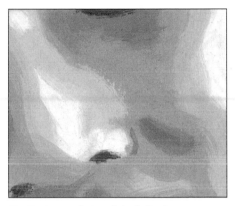

5. Paint white highlights on the nose, cheek and mouth. Add touches of brown on the nostrils, down one side of the face and under the chin.

6. Mix colors for the hair and clothes, and paint them. Lastly, add details on the eyes and lips with a fine brush.

31

Warm and cold colors

You don't have to use natural-looking colors and shading to paint faces. Instead, you can create shapes by using the contrasts between warm, reddish colors and cold, bluish colors, as in the painting on the right. This face, by artist, Alexej von Jawlensky, is made up of solid blocks of color.

Yellows, oranges and reds are the colors of fire and the sun, so they are called warm colors. They look bright and stand out against other colors. Purples, blues and greens are the colors of water and ice, so they are called cold colors. Things painted in them look like they are in shadow and also seem more distant.

> 👁 To see how artists use warm and cold colors, go to: **www.utah.edu/umfa/olsen.html** and click on the colors in the painting. Find out how warm and cold colors can represent feelings at: **members.aol.com/Sabbeth/Color.html** For quick links to these sites, go to: **www.usborne-quicklinks.com**

Head of a young girl, by Alexej von Jawlensky. This painting contrasts warm oranges and reds with cold blues and black.

1. Draw a large, simple face in pencil. Connect one eyebrow to the top of the nose. Add lines between the nose and chin.

2. Mix some bright orange acrylic paint. Paint the whole face orange. Leave it for a few minutes to dry.

3. When the paint has dried, use a thin brush to go over your pencil lines again in blue acrylic paint, like this.

32

4. Paint dark shadows around the features in purple. On the cheeks and eyes, use green. The upper lip is purple and green.

5. Paint the lower lip and pupils in red. Use more red at the top of the ear and on the cheeks and forehead.

6. Use yellow for the lightest areas like the highlights on the nose and lips. Paint the "whites" of the eyes yellow.

★ Paint a light background color to set off the bright acrylic colors.

Watercolors

Watercolor paints are ideal for adding color to a pen or pencil drawing. You can use them to create gradual blends or bold splashes of color without covering up your original drawing. The paints come as blocks or tubes, and need to be mixed with water before you use them.

Watercolor tubes

Watercolor blocks are called pans.

Using watercolors

With blocks, wet your brush and rub it over a block until its tip is covered in paint. Dab the paint onto a plate.

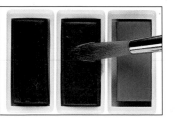

With tubes, squeeze a little bit of paint out onto a plate. Then, add water gradually with your brush.

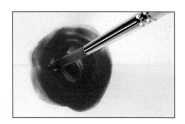

Wet watercolors blur together.

If you don't want colors to blur, wait for each one to dry before adding the next.

The more water you add, the paler the color will be.

Pen and watercolor face

These steps show you how to use pen and watercolors together in a quick, simple style. Use a pen with permanent ink (see page 18), or your drawing will smudge when you paint over it. This style looks best if you work quickly, so don't worry about painting neat shapes.

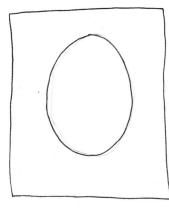

1. Draw a rectangle with a ballpoint pen or a permanent marker. Add an oval.

2. Draw in simple eyes, nose, mouth, ears and eyebrows. Don't worry if they look uneven.

3. Draw a curved line for the shoulders. Add two straight lines for the neck.

4. Draw a few lines for the hair. The lines can be straight or wavy, and long or short.

34

5. Mix a skin tone using red and orange. Roughly paint the face, making one side darker than the other.

6. Paint one side of the hair yellow, and the other side orange. Add more orange to both sides by the neck.

7. Paint the body and background. Make them both darker on the right-hand side, like the face and hair.

★ This technique works well with a stylized face (see pages 12-13).

★ Try drawing a landscape in the background.

★ Add touches of color for the lips, cheeks and eyes. Let the colors blur into the rest of the face.

Cartoons

A cartoon face is simpler than a real face, but you can build it up in a similar way. The steps below show you how.

👁 For step-by-step lessons on drawing cartoons, go to: **www.cartooncorner.com/artsfolder/howtacartoon/ cartooning.html** and click on "Begin the lessons". For a quick link to this site, go to: **www.usborne-quicklinks.com**

Simple paint cartoons

This oval was painted using watercolors.

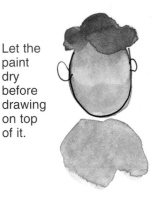

Let the paint dry before drawing on top of it.

1. Mix a watery skin tone using orange and pink paint. Paint a rough oval shape for the face.

2. Mix another color for the body of your cartoon. Paint a patch of it below the oval, like this.

3. Mix a color for the hair. Paint a patch on top of the oval. Don't worry if it blurs into the oval.

4. Draw a line around the bottom of the oval in pen. Add roundish ears half-way down each side.

Try different clothes and poses.

5. Add two dots for eyes, level with the tops of the ears. Add curved lines for the nose and the mouth.

6. Draw a few lines over the hair. Use curly, wavy or straight lines for different kinds of hair.

7. Draw a scarf, if you like. Then, draw curved lines for the shoulders. Add two lines to make arms.

8. Try creating more cartoon characters using different shapes and colors for the face, body and hair.

Cartoon expressions

A cartoon expression depends on how you draw the eyes, eyebrows and mouth. Cartoon expressions are similar to real expressions (see pages 40-41), but they are simpler and exaggerated to make them look funny.

Experiment with different ways of drawing features, to see what expressions you can create.

★ Download these faces to color in from: **www.usborne-quicklinks.com**

Different shapes

You can use different shapes to draw cartoon faces and features. Experiment with shapes to see what characters you can create.

Try drawing faces on squares, rectangles or triangles.

Add hats or glasses to your cartoons.

★ Download these faces to color in from: **www.usborne-quicklinks.com**

A cartoon crowd

A crowd is an interesting way to put different faces together. Start with a row of cartoons near the bottom of your paper. Give them all different clothes, hair and expressions. Add more rows behind them. Make some of the faces look at each other.

The faces in this crowd were drawn using different colors, shapes and expressions, so each one looks different.

Color contrasts

Colors that contrast strongly with each other look brighter together than on their own. Pairs of colors called complementary colors (see below) have the strongest contrasts. Seen together, complementary colors look so bright they almost seem to glow.

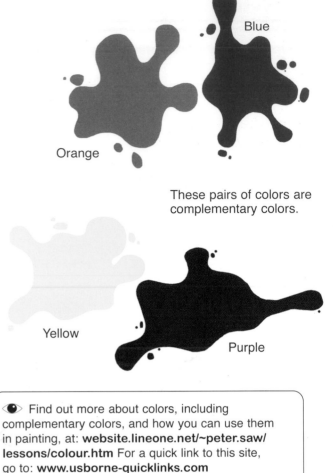

These pairs of colors are complementary colors.

Complementary colors

There are three pairs of complementary colors: red and green, orange and blue, and yellow and purple. Each primary color (red, yellow or blue) has a complementary color that you get by mixing the other two primary colors. For example, the complementary of red is green, which is made by mixing yellow and blue.

👁 Find out more about colors, including complementary colors, and how you can use them in painting, at: **website.lineone.net/~peter.saw/ lessons/colour.htm** For a quick link to this site, go to: **www.usborne-quicklinks.com**

Using complementary colors

This project shows you how to use wax crayons and watercolors in complementary colors to create a striking, mask-style face.

You will need crayons in orange, purple and green, as well as watercolors in their complementary colors: blue, yellow and red.

1. Draw a simple face with faint pencil lines. Use curved lines to divide the face into separate areas.

2. Go over your drawing with orange, purple and green crayons. Use a different color to outline each area of the face.

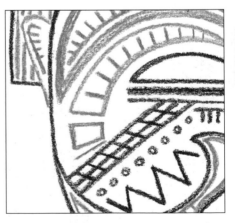

3. Using the same crayon colors, add patterns of circles and lines to decorate each area of the face.

The shapes and patterns in this face were based on an African mask.

4. Put patches of blue, yellow and red watercolor on your plate. Don't make the paint too wet, so the colors stay bright.

The wax repels the paint and shows through.

5. Paint each area of the face in its complementary color. For example, paint a shape with an orange outline in blue.

This small face was drawn using red, yellow and blue crayons, then painted with orange, purple and green paints.

Add a neck and shoulders if you like.

Expressions

Thirty-six Faces of Expression, by Louis Leopold Boilly. This painting shows a range of extreme expressions, including thoughtful, sad, surprised and angry.

👁 See how to draw cartoon-style expressions at: **www.polykarbon.com/tutorials/expression/expression.htm** For a quick link to this site, go to: **www.usborne-quicklinks.com**

Every time you draw a face, you draw an expression. An expression affects the whole face, not just the eyes and mouth. Most portraits show people smiling or being serious, but there are many other expressions you could try – there are over 30 just in the picture above.

1. Find a picture of a face with a striking expression. Put a piece of tracing paper over it and outline the face.

2. Trace the lines made by the eyebrows, eyes and mouth, and the creases in the skin around them. These are the lines you need to create an expression.

40

Try tracing other faces to see what lines you get from different expressions.

Expression lines are useful for drawing cartoons, too (see pages 36-37).

Sneering

Happy

 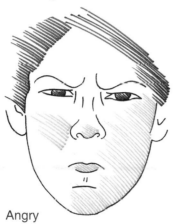

Angry

Bored

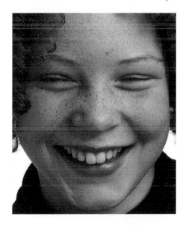 

Laughing

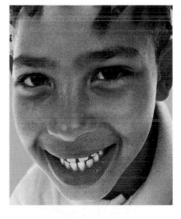 

Smiling

 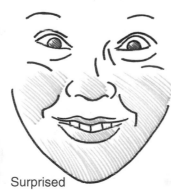

Surprised

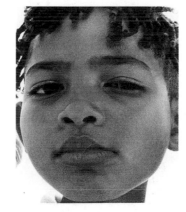 

Proud

41

Distorting faces

Distorting a face is an interesting way to produce caricatures or fantasy faces. You can use a grid, as shown on the next page, or draw a distorted reflection. Alternatively, you could try drawing a face based on the distorted faces at the bottom of this page.

Distorted reflections

Any object with a shiny, curved surface will give you a distorted reflection. Try looking at the side of a saucepan or the back of a spoon. The picture on the right shows the reflection in a shiny ball – you could use a Christmas decoration. The closer you are to the object, the more distorted your reflection will be.

Try distorting the faces at: **www.magixl.com/ caric./profil/gallery.html** Click on "Next one, please" for more faces. For a quick link to this site, go to: **www.usborne-quicklinks.com**

Hand with reflecting sphere, by M.C. Escher. This is an example of an artist using distortion to draw himself and the room around him.

These three faces were distorted using a computer program called Adobe® Photoshop®.

You could use these faces as references.

Distorting a face using a grid

Using a grid allows you to distort a face in many ways, depending on how you draw the grid. Widely-spaced gridlines stretch features, while closely-spaced lines squash them. Find a picture you can draw over, such as a magazine picture or a drawing you've already done.

Make the lines very faint.

1. Use a pencil and ruler to mark out a grid of 1" squares over your picture. Count the squares along both edges.

2. Then, draw a new grid with the same number of squares. Use wavy lines instead of straight ones and space them out unevenly.

3. Count the squares to the chin on the original picture. Draw it in the same position on the new grid. Do the same for the sides of the face.

4. Look at the original picture to see where the features are. Match these squares with the new grid and draw them in.

5. Draw in the hair, making it follow the shape of the gridlines. When you have finished drawing the face, shade it in.

You don't need to draw the distorted features and face shape too exactly to get a good effect.

The face below was stretched in the middle.

You can get a very different result by drawing a different grid shape in step 2.

Caricatures

A caricature looks like the person it shows, but it alters and exaggerates their features to make them look funny. You often see caricatures of famous people in newspapers.

Tracing caricature

These steps show you how to draw a caricature with tracing paper, starting with a face from a magazine picture or a photograph. If you can, find a face with striking features. It will be easier to caricature. This face has big eyes, wide cheeks and pouting lips.

This caricature was painted with watercolors.

1. Place a piece of tracing paper over the photograph. You can use masking tape to hold it in place. Make a tracing of the face.

2. Starting with the face shape, trace your tracing. Draw outside your original lines to make the cheeks wider and the chin narrower.

3. Trace the features. Alter them a little, but don't draw as far outside the original lines. The lips and eyes are just slightly bigger.

4. Alter the hair. In this example, the bangs are shorter and the ends flip up more. Copy the finished face onto a new piece of paper.

Every face is different, and can be altered in different ways to make a caricature. Here is another example.

1. Start by making an accurate tracing of the photograph, as described in step 1 on the previous page.

2. Trace the tracing, starting at the top. The hair is spikier, the forehead squarer and the eyebrows thicker.

3. To make the face longer, move the tracing up slightly, then trace and enlarge the nose and chin.

★ This caricature was drawn in pen and then painted.

4. Finish the tracing, making the smile bigger. Copy the face onto a new piece of paper and color it in.

👁 You can see caricatures of famous actors, pop stars, and sportsmen and women at the Caricature Zone. Go to: **www.magixl.com/heads/view.html** and click on one of the names on the list. For a quick link to this site, go to: **www.usborne-quick links.com**

Paper collage

Collage comes from the French word "coller," which means to stick. A paper collage is a picture made by gluing down scraps of different papers.

👁 Artists make collages from lots of different things, including newspapers and photographs. For some more ideas of things you can use to make collages, go to: **www.kidsart.com/tt101099.html** For a quick link to this site, go to: **www.usborne-quicklinks.com**

Rip colored paper out of magazines.

Sort papers by color, so they're easier to use.

Keep scraps of wrapping paper, too.

A collage face

Look through old magazines for different colored papers. Collect papers in the colors you need to make a face: flesh tones and colors for the eyes, hair, background and clothes. You will need lighter and darker tones of each color, to create a shaded effect.

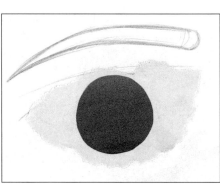

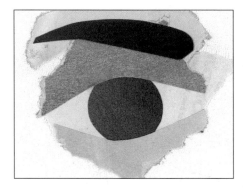

1. Draw a face in pencil. Keep the shapes simple and don't shade it in. Decide what colors you are going to use.

2. For each eye, tear an almond shape in off-white paper. Stick it down. Cut out a colored circle and glue it on top.

3. Tear a gray eyelid and a pale crescent to go under the eye. Trim the inner edges. Cut an eyebrow from dark paper.

4. Tear strips in light and dark skin tones for the nose. Fill in the forehead, cheeks and chin with more torn pieces.

5. Cut out a dark red upper lip. Cut out a lower lip in dark pink. Add some dark flesh tones around the lips.

6. Add small, white highlights on the eyes. Then fill in the clothes, background and hair with different colors.

For the hair, tear strips out of
magazine pictures of real hair.

Use big, torn
pieces for the
background.

Use a
contrasting
color for the
clothes.

Pastel scratch

For a colorful, textured picture, you can use this scratched oil pastel technique. This involves scraping lines into a layer of black ink to reveal bright, oil pastel colors underneath. You will need oil pastels, a bottle of black permanent ink, a brush, a pencil, a black felt-tip pen and a sheet of Bristol paper. You will also need something to scrape with, such as the end of a small screwdriver or the nib of a dip pen.

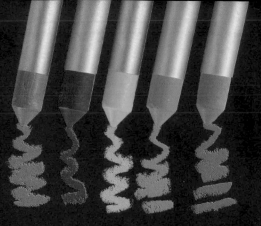

Oil pastels give bright, strong colors that show up well against black.

A pastel scratch face

1. Draw a head and shoulders in pencil. Decorate the background. Go over your picture with thick, pen lines.

2. Color in your picture with bright oil pastels. Use orange and yellow for the skin. Leave the pen lines showing through.

3. Color the mouth in red and the whites of the eyes in white. Choose another bright color like green for the hair.

4. Choose more bright colors for the clothes and background. The colors don't have to be realistic.

5. When you have finished filling in your drawing, brush a layer of black ink evenly over the whole picture.

6. When the ink is dry, scrape lines through it to reveal your drawing. Vary the direction of your lines as you scrape.

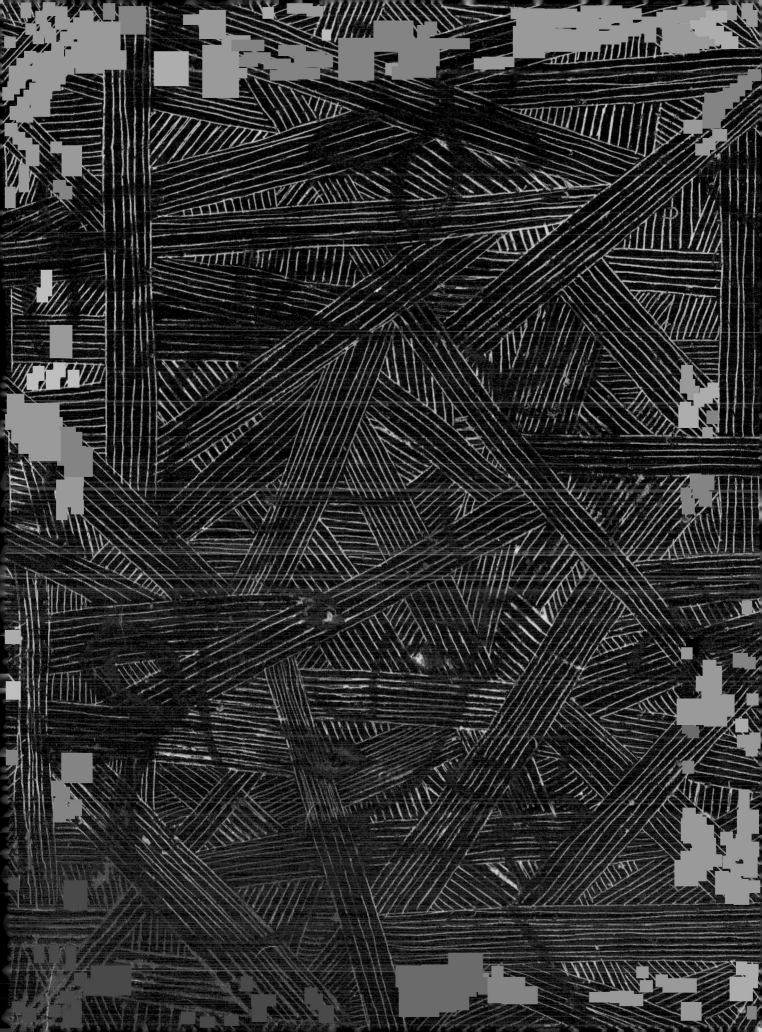

Printing

These pages show you how to print faces using paper stencils. This means cutting your picture out of paper and printing it by sponging paint through the holes. Stencils suit simple, bold pictures with clear shapes and bright colors, like the prints by Andy Warhol below.

These prints were made by artist, Andy Warhol. They are self-portraits. Warhol used bold shapes and colors to create a striking image that he repeated lots of times. This kind of picture is sometimes called "Pop Art".

👁 To see more prints by Warhol, go to: **martinlawrence. com/warhol.html** and click on the picture names. For a quick link to this site, go to: **www.usborne-quicklinks.com**

Drawing a picture

Take a piece of paper and draw a 1" border around the edges. Draw a face in the middle using solid shapes you will be able to cut out. Keep it simple – your finished print can only have a few colors.

You may need to simplify the face again, for example, on the eyes.

Choosing colors

Choose four bright colors to fill in the main areas of color in your picture. For dark areas, use blue or black. Be aware that the colors you print will change slightly when you print one color on top of another.

Try out color combinations by coloring over your drawing.

Making the stencils

You need to make a separate stencil for each of the colors in your picture. To make the stencils, you will need five sheets of Bristol paper, a pencil and a craft knife. You will also need a piece of old cardboard to press on while using the knife.

Tape your drawing to a window so the light makes it easier to trace.

1. Make five copies of your drawing on Bristol paper. Trace it carefully, making sure both pieces of paper line up neatly along the edges.

2. For each color, take one copy of your drawing and outline the parts which will be that color. This will be the area you cut out.

3. Lay each stencil one at a time on the cardboard. Cut carefully around your outlines with a craft knife. See page 59 for tips on using a craft knife.

As well as the stencil for the skin, shown in step 3, this print uses stencils for the hair, eyes, shadows, lips, shoulders, and the glasses.

★ You can print out the templates for all the stencils needed to make this print from: **www.usborne-quicklinks.com**

Printing the stencils

To print your picture, you will need some masking tape, several sheets of colored paper to print on, acrylic or poster paints, and an old sponge cut into small pieces. Printing can be a little messy, so cover your table with old newspapers before you start.

You build up the finished picture in stages. Each color is printed separately, using one stencil at a time. It is important to line up the edges of each stencil with the edges of your paper, or the colored areas won't line up on the finished print. You can use masking tape to hold the stencils in place while you print.

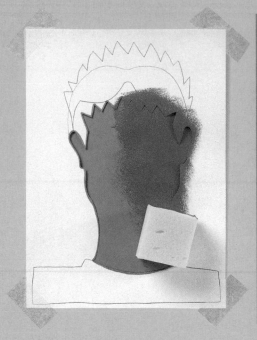

The paint will take several minutes to dry.

1. Tape the skin stencil over a piece of paper. Put some pink paint on an old plate. Dip a sponge in the paint, then dab it over the gaps in the stencil.

2. Lift off the stencil. While you wait for the paint to dry, start some more prints using the same stencil on the different colors of paper.

Make sure each layer of paint is dry before you apply the next.

3. When the paint is dry, tape the next stencil over your paper. Dab the next color of paint over the stencil with another piece of sponge.

4. Repeat the process with the other stencils to finish your print. Then, finish the other prints. If you like, you can vary the colors on each print.

5. When all your prints have dried, you could pick the four best ones and tape them together to make one big picture (see right).

52

Sculpted faces

You can cut and shape paper to make a three-dimensional, sculpted face. To make one, you will need Bristol paper to make the shapes, and cardboard for backing. You will also need a pencil and eraser, scissors, glue, a ruler, an old piece of cardboard to cut on, and a craft knife (see page 59 for tips on using a craft knife safely before you begin).

The shapes in this picture have been scored and then folded (see top right).

★ You can print out the templates for all the shapes needed to make this face from: **www.usborne-quicklinks.com**

Scoring and folding

Score lines

Alternate folds create pleats.

Draw faint lines as guides for scoring.

Follow the shape of the curve as you pinch.

1. Cut out a rectangle of thick paper. Score lines on it by running a craft knife gently over the paper without cutting through it.

2. Fold the paper along one line. Run your nail over the fold. Fold it the other way along the next line. Fold all the lines alternate ways.

3. To score and fold wavy lines, cut out a shape like this. Draw three wavy lines on it. Score gently along the lines with a craft knife.

4. Gradually pinch the paper along a line to get a curved fold. Turn it over and pinch the next line. Turn it back to pinch the last line.

A paper face

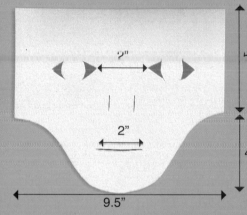

2"

2"

5"

4"

9.5"

1. Draw this face shape on Bristol paper. Cut it out. Cut out holes for the eyes and slits for the nose and mouth.

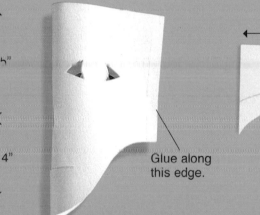

Glue along this edge.

2. Bend the face shape in half, without making a sharp fold, and glue the edges together. Hold it until the glue is dry.

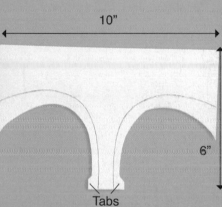

10"

6"

Tabs

3. Draw this shape for the nose and forehead. Cut it out. Score the two lines shown. Fold the paper along them.

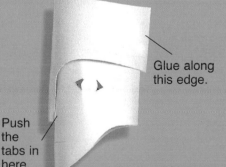

Glue along this edge.

Push the tabs in here.

4. Push the nose tabs into the slits on the face shape. Bend the forehead around and glue the edges onto the face shape.

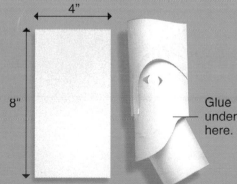

4"

8"

Glue under here.

5. Cut a rectangle. Bend it in half without creasing and glue the short edges together. Glue it at an angle inside the face.

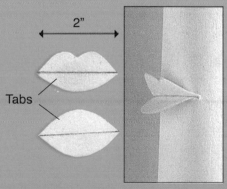

2"

Tabs

6. For the lips, cut out two pieces like this. Fold them in the middle and push the tabs into the slit for the mouth.

You don't have to follow the hair sizes and shapes exactly.

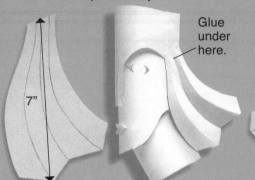

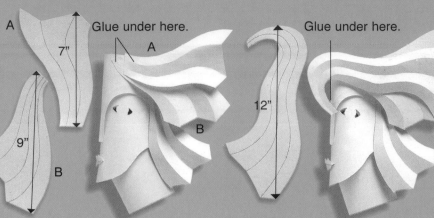

Glue under here.

A
7"

A

B

9"

B

Glue under here.

7"

Glue under here.

Glue under here.

12"

7. For the hair, draw and cut out a shape like this. Score and fold it along the lines. Glue it at the side of the face shape.

8. Cut out and score two more shapes in the same way. Arrange them at the top of the face and glue them on.

9. Cut and score a long shape. Place it over the rest of the hair. Tuck the tip behind the forehead and glue it in place.

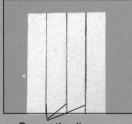

12"

Glue under here.

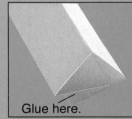

2.5"

Score this line.

Glue under here.

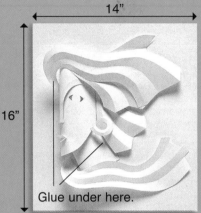

14"

16"

Glue under here.

10. Cut and score a long shape for the scarf. Place it on the neck. Tuck the tip behind the neck and glue it in place.

11. Cut out a curly earring. Score and fold it along the line shown. Glue the middle of the curl onto the hair.

12. Cut out a rectangle of cardboard for the backing. Arrange the face in the middle of the rectangle. Glue it down.

Framing the face

Score the lines 0.5" apart.

Glue here.

Fold the paper so the end makes a triangle.

The strips fit together like this at the corners.

1. Cut out two rectangles of paper, each 14" x 2", and two rectangles of 15" x 2". Score three lines down each.

2. Make each rectangle into a triangular strip by folding all the lines the same way. Glue the overlapping sides together.

3. Glue the shorter strips at the top and bottom of the backing. Glue the long strips so they fit in between.

56

Different views

Not all faces follow the basic shapes described on pages 6-7. The shape of a face changes according to the angle you see it from. These pages show you how a face changes when someone looks up or down, or sideways.

For step-by-step instructions on drawing a cartoon-style face looking to the side (called a "three-quarter view"), go to: **www.polykarbon.com/tutorials/newface/3quarter 1.htm** Click on "Next" to see the final steps. For a quick link to this site, go to: **www.usborne-quicklinks.com**

Looking up and down

The guidelines explained on pages 6-7 work for a front view of a face. When someone looks up or down, the guideline for the eyes moves up or down too (see right), although you can still use the central guideline for the nose. The features look different, too.

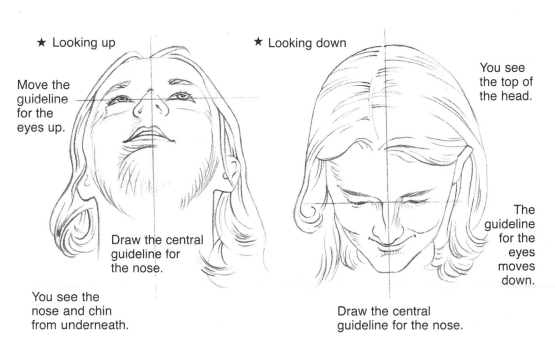

★ Looking up

Move the guideline for the eyes up.

Draw the central guideline for the nose.

You see the nose and chin from underneath.

★ Looking down

You see the top of the head.

The guideline for the eyes moves down.

Draw the central guideline for the nose.

Looking left and right

The pictures below show you how to draw different views as someone turns their head. As with looking up and down, some of the basic guidelines from pages 6-7 still work, but not all of them. The shapes and spacing of the features is different, too.

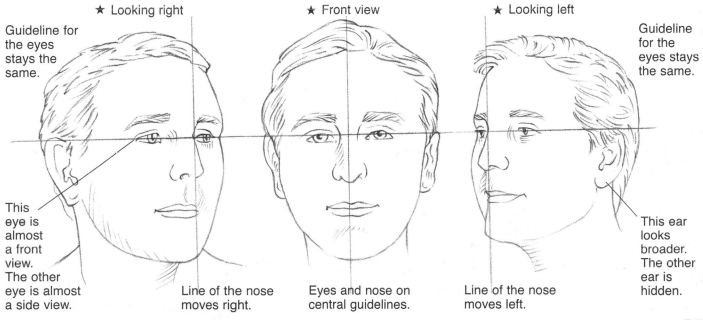

★ Looking right

Guideline for the eyes stays the same.

This eye is almost a front view. The other eye is almost a side view.

Line of the nose moves right.

★ Front view

Eyes and nose on central guidelines.

★ Looking left

Guideline for the eyes stays the same.

This ear looks broader. The other ear is hidden.

Line of the nose moves left.

Techniques and tips

The techniques and tips on these pages will help you draw better pictures of faces, especially if you are drawing someone sitting in front of you. There are also some useful practical hints.

👁 Find out how to use "thumbnail" sketches to try out ideas and plan drawings at: **www.sanford-artedventures. com/create/tech_thumbnails.html** For easy access to this site, go to: **www.usborne-quicklinks.com**

Different lighting

When you are drawing someone, you can change how they look by using different lighting. Here are some ideas to try. Experiment with the lighting before you start drawing, until you find an effect you like. Try combining lighting effects with different poses, too.

Side lighting creates dramatic highlights and shadows on the face.

This is a profile lit from the front of the face, making the back of the head very dark.

Lighting from below, from a desk lamp or flashlight, creates a spooky effect.

Lighting from below can look scary when combined with a dark background.

Checking drawings

You can use a pencil to check how features line up with each other. This is particularly helpful when you are drawing a face at an angle.

To check how someone's features line up from left to right, hold a pencil vertically with your arm straight out in front of you, and shut one eye.

To check how the features line up from top to bottom, hold a pencil horizontally. Look at your drawing and check the features you have drawn line up.

The left side of the nose lines up with the left corner of the mouth.

The bottom of the nose lines up with the top of the lips.

Extra features

When drawing a face, you might want to add extra features such as glasses, jewelry or makeup. Here are some tips on how to draw them.

Draw glasses after you have drawn the eyes.

For a mouth with lipstick, use dark shading on the lips.

Shade the background to show up light-colored hair.

Leave a white highlight to make an earring look shiny.

You don't need to shade right to the edges of your paper.

Fixing drawings

If you use soft pencils, chalk pastels or charcoal, it's best to fix your drawing by spraying it with fixative spray or hairspray. This seals the surface of the picture so it won't smudge. Do the spraying somewhere with lots of fresh air.

Go over your picture with horizontal sweeps of spray, following the directions on the can or bottle. Then go over the picture again with vertical sweeps. Leave it for a few minutes to dry.

Don't use too much spray.

Cutting tips

Craft knives are very sharp, so follow these tips to use one safely:

• Protect your table by putting an old piece of thick cardboard under what you are cutting.

• While cutting, always keep your fingers away from the sharp blade of the knife.

• Press gently. If you don't cut all the way through the first time, just go over the cut again.

• For straight cuts or score lines, use a metal ruler. Keep your fingers away from its edge.

Gallery

Over the next four pages you can see a gallery of faces, all drawn using methods and materials explained in this book. Look through the faces for new ideas. Turn back to the pages given to read more about each method.

★ Try making quick drawings using smudged pen shading (see pages 18-19).

★ This face was shaded with oil pastels as on page 25, then finished with blue outlines, dark hair and a beard.

★ For this spooky lighting effect, the model held a flashlight pointing at his chin (see page 58).

★ The stylized face above was drawn and colored with chalk pastels (see page 26).

60

For a scene like this, make the background with large pieces of tissue paper. Then, add the faces on top (see pages 12-13).

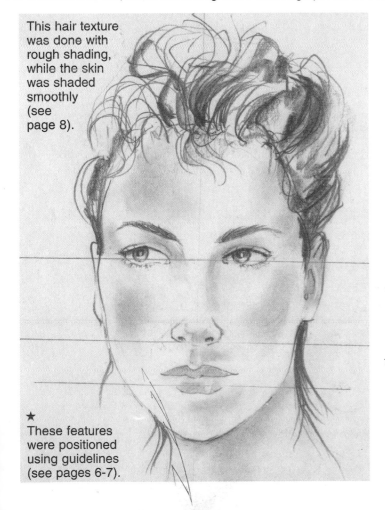

This hair texture was done with rough shading, while the skin was shaded smoothly (see page 8).

★ These features were positioned using guidelines (see pages 6-7).

★ This caricature was drawn from a painting called the Mona Lisa. See pages 44-45 for more about caricatures.

👁 See pictures by children from around the world at: **www.naturalchild.com/gallery/** Click on the down arrow below "Select Page" and choose a page number, then click on "Go!" to get to that page. For a quick link to this site, go to: **www.usborne-quicklinks.com**

See faces from all over the world at: **www.artsmia.org/face-to-face/** Click on "Enter the Gallery of Faces," then on the pictures to see large versions. For a quick link to this site, go to: **www.usborne-quicklinks.com**

★ The face above was drawn on a computer using the brush and shape tools (see pages 14-17).

★ This face was painted with acrylics in warm and cold colors (see pages 32-33).

★ These cartoons were drawn in pen, each with a different expression (see page 36).

★ This picture was drawn using only curvy lines, then shaded with colored pencils (see pages 10-11).

★ The striking expression lines on this face were copied from a photograph (see pages 40-41).

62

★ To draw the dramatic black and white picture above, the face was divided into areas of light and dark, as on pages 30-31, but with only two tones.

★ Try making paint cartoons (see pages 36-37) with wild hair styles or dramatic expressions.

★ The picture below uses the scratched oil pastel technique from pages 48-49, done with pink, blue, yellow and green pastels.

★ The face above was drawn in pen, then painted with watercolors (see page 18).

★ To paint like this, use watercolors (see page 34) with a very soft brush.

63

Index

B

*JQ
743.4
Dickins*

Acknowledgements

Every effort has been made to trace the copyright holders of the material in this book. If any rights have been omitted, the publishers offer their sincere apologies and will rectify this in any subsequent editions following notification. The publishers are grateful to the following organizations and individuals for their contributions and permission to reproduce material:

Page 5. Vincent Van Gogh: 'Self-Portrait' (1889) oil on canvas © Gianni Dagli Orti/CORBIS.
Page 5. Leonardo Da Vinci: 'La Scapigliata' © Archivo Iconografico, S.A./CORBIS.
Page 10. David Hockney: 'Manolo. London' (1977) crayon on paper 10" x 8" © David Hockney.
Page 22. Pablo Picasso: 'Portrait of Dora Maar' (1937) oil on canvas © Succession Picasso/DACS 2001. Musée Picasso/SuperStock.
Page 32. Alexej von Jawlensky: 'Head of Young Girl (Madchenkopf)'oil on board © DACS 2001. Christie's/SuperStock.
Page 40. Louis Leopold Boilly: 'Thirty-six Faces of Expression' © Explorer, Paris/SuperStock.
Page 42. M.C. Escher's "Hand with Reflecting Sphere" © 2000 Cordon Art B.V. - Baarn - Holland. All rights reserved.
Page 50. Andy Warhol: Six Self-portraits (1967) © The Andy Warhol Foundation for the Visual Arts, Inc./ARS, NY and DACS, London 2001. Bettmann/CORBIS.
Screen shots on pages 14-17 used with permission from Microsoft Corporation. Microsoft®, Microsoft®Windows®95, Windows®98, Windows®2000 and Microsoft®Paint are either registered Trade Marks or Trade Marks of Microsoft Corporation in the US and other countries. Quicktime is a Trade Mark of Apple Computer, Inc. Shockwave® is a Trade Mark of Macromedia. RealPlayer® is a Trade Mark of RealNetworks. Adobe® and Adobe®Photoshop® are Trade Marks of Adobe Systems, Inc.

Picture researcher: Ruth King. Photographic manipulation by John Russell. Thanks to Brian Voakes.